KU-522-775

1 INTRODUCTION

MORE FOR LESS

I want you to deliver **more:**
- Profit
- Sales
- Productivity
- Customers
- Quality

And, by the way, you've got **less:**
- Money
- Staff
- Time
- Machinery

Sounds familiar? Year on year, managers are being asked to get more results from fewer resources or, at least, more from the same. All too often, there is little guidance on how to achieve this. So, where do you begin?

ROUTE TO IMPROVING EFFICIENCY

6. Check customer perception
 - How effective have your
   efforts been?
 - How can you tell?

1. Understand your operation
 - Do you know your operation
   well enough to improve it?

5. Continuously improve
 - Do you have a
   systematic approach
   to constant improvement?

2. Set the right objectives
 - Do you have the right
   objectives to steer
   improvement?

4. Increase capacity
 - Are you meeting demand?
 - What action(s) can you take?
 - How efficient are your resources?

3. Improve work processing
 - How can you identify non-value-
   added (wasteful) activity?
 - How can you remove it?

IMPROVING EFFICIENCY

This pocketbook will help all managers in their efforts to get **more for less** or **more for the same level of resources** – this is our simple definition of efficiency (more later).

Today's organisations and management responsibilities are highly diverse and yet the tools of process improvement tie them together. So, no matter whether your work relates to managing an office or retail outlet, or the manufacture of space shuttles, you'll find tools here that will help your operation.

Consistent and systematic application of the tools and techniques provided will improve both the efficiency and effectiveness of your processes and resources. In addition, this will help build more effective relationships between divisions and departments within any organisation.

The **efficient** production of goods and services, valued by customers and delivered to the **highest possible standards**, inevitably results in greater competitive advantage.

1. Understand your operation
- Do you know your operation
  well enough to improve it?

2. Set the right objectives
- Do you have the right
  objectives to steer

UNDERSTAND YOUR OPERATION

THE OPERATIONS MODEL

The Operations Model is the building block for understanding your operation.

Inputs	Process	Outputs

Inputs go into a process

- People (customers and employees)
- Materials (raw materials, components, applications, etc)
- Information (objectives, standards, computer data, phone calls, etc)
- Facilities (buildings, computers, machinery, etc)

Outputs result from the process

- Products or services (both good and bad - we need to avoid the 'bad')
- Waste (mistakes that cannot be recycled/recovered from – we need to prevent these)
- Scrap (errors that can be rectified at a price – we need to reduce these)

A process 'transforms' inputs through various activities into outputs.
Why is this transformation of interest? Because all transformations should **add value** if they are to be profitable. What value do **your** processes add? (See page 43).

TRANSFORMING INPUTS

Processes transform inputs in four main ways:

1. **Alteration** – inputs can be combined or changed.
- Car assembly lines bring components together to make a car
- Steel factories combine raw materials to create steel

Many manufacturing processes primarily focus on alteration.

2. **Inspection** – inputs can be checked to ensure a standard is reached or reviewed against certain criteria.
- Mortgage lenders inspect and approve applications
- Solicitors confirm legal conditions are met

Many service industries focus on inspection skills.

3. **Transportation** – inputs often need moving from where they currently are, to where the need for them exists.
- The post office moves letters from sender to receiver
- Security companies move cash from banks to wage offices

4. **Storage** – inputs are often not needed immediately, so require storing.
- Hotels provide a bed overnight for people to sleep
- Warehouses keep goods until demanded by customers

Why are you interested in the transformation? Because all transformations should **add value** if they are to be profitable!

(7)

UNDERSTAND YOUR OPERATION

A CREDIT CARD EXAMPLE

Consider an application for a credit card:

Inputs	Process	Outputs
A customer submits an application.	A process takes place which receives the application, **inspects*** it, compares it to certain criteria and if acceptable ...	Issues a credit card or rejects the application if unsuitable.

*It's the inspection skills that are important in this example.
Why is that? Hint: Who would lose and how, if someone with a poor
credit risk was given a high credit limit? See our comments at the end of this chapter.

UNDERSTAND YOUR OPERATION

PROCESS CHAINS

A process usually consists of a chain of operations, each one probably done by different people, different departments, perhaps in different buildings or countries!

The output (O) of each operation forms an input (I) to the next.

In our seemingly simple credit card example, eight operations could be involved:

1. The **post room** receives the application and *sends* it to the

2. **Data entry team** whose computer system *connects* to an

3. **External credit agency** database whose findings are *reviewed* by the

4. **Credit checking team** and a decision to accept or reject is made. *Card details for successful applicants are automatically sent to the*

5. **Card production system** from where the embossed cards *go* to the

6. **Print room** where letters are printed, matched with cards, enveloped, batched and *passed* to the

7. **Post room** for franking and dispatch. Applications are *stored* by the

8. **Archive team** and are *requested* by **customer services** in the event of a query/complaint.

CUSTOMER-SUPPLIER CHAINS

Drawing your own process **'chain'** forces you to identify your **suppliers (S)** and your **customers (C)**.

If your operation is the first one in the chain, then your suppliers are probably outside your company. If you're the last operation in a process then your customer is probably another business or 'the man on the street'. Most of us are, however, part of an **internal customer-supplier** chain in that we are customers of the previous operation and suppliers to the next.

We need to manage better all the interfaces in internal chains if we are to avoid waste, excess cost, re-work, political in-fighting and the other non-value-added activities. Considering some simple questions can help you to avoid these problems and build better internal relationships. See the Internal Customer and Supplier Checklists on the next two pages.

UNDERSTAND YOUR OPERATION

INTERNAL CUSTOMER CHECKLIST

Hewlett-Packard's Queensferry, UK plant developed the following simple, but highly effective, checklist which was adopted throughout H-P's world-wide operations.

1. Who are my customers?
2. What do they need?
3. What is my product/service?
4. What are my customers' expectations and measures?
5. Does my product or service meet their expectations?
6. What is the process for providing my product or service?
7. What action is required to improve the process?

Produced with the permission of Hewlett-Packard

INTERNAL SUPPLIER CHECKLIST

We can also usefully apply an internal supplier checklist to help ensure that we get what we need for our process.

1. Who are our suppliers?
2. What do we need from them?
3. What resources do they provide us with?
4. What are our expectations and measures?
5. Do the resources supplied to us meet our expectations?
6. What is the process for acquiring the resources?
7. What action is required to improve the process?
8. Do we understand our supplier's process?
9. What can we do to help them to improve their process?

UNDERSTAND YOUR OPERATION

KEEP CUSTOMERS & SUPPLIERS HAPPY

Your internal customers and suppliers can't just walk away if they're dissatisfied with you, or you with them. To resolve operational issues you must **work together**.

Using the Internal Customer and Supplier Checklists can help you to define or improve:

- **Service Level Agreements:** can you agree/quantify what you need from each other?
- **Common Performance Measures:** to ensure that you are pulling in the same direction, so the success of one will not harm the other.
- **Communication:** be open/honest, think 'WIN WIN'; often all you need do is **TALK!**

External customers don't work for your organisation and today it's easier than ever for them to choose another supplier if you don't satisfy them. Close co-operation is needed between Operations and Marketing to ensure the external customer is kept satisfied. The interface between these two functions is critical to efficiency improvement.

Working together should, for example, prevent Marketing designing forms that Operations can't process quickly, or Operations requesting information in a language customers can't understand.

BACK TO OUR CREDIT CARD EXAMPLE

Remember our credit card example on page 8?
We asked you why 'inspection'
was important.

This transformation activity aims to
assess whether data is complete,
relevant and accurate, so allowing
accurate assessment of the
applicant's creditworthiness, cards
to be issued with the correct name
details and valuable marketing data
to be collated. Failure to do that
successfully could result in financial
loss for the issuer if the applicant runs
up debts that cannot be repaid.

- Do you know your operation
  well enough to improve it?

2. Set the right objectives
- Do you have the right
  objectives to steer
  improvement?

3. Improve work processing
  - How can you identify non-value-

NON-ALIGNED OBJECTIVES

With traditional approaches to efficiency improvement, functions and departments are, too often, treated in isolation from each other. As a result, they each set their own objectives and have their own measures of success and, some cynics would say, their own hidden agenda.

You can guess the result – at best lacklustre improvement but, at worst, lasting damage can be done to customer relations and business results. Warning signs are:

- Inter-departmental rivalry – 'us and them'; departments retreat to their 'fox-holes' and take shots at each other
- No sense of direction – lack of accountability for process improvement across departmental boundaries
- Major communication breakdowns (eg: a marketing campaign that Operations are unaware of)

Who cares about the customer?!

The effect is a self-destructive mix of indifference, ignorance and arrogance toward the customer.

How can we ignore that we work in the same organisation and for the same customers!!!

ALIGNMENT OF OBJECTIVES IS VITAL

How will success in your objectives help deliver the Business Vision?

How do strategic decisions affect your ability to deliver customer satisfaction?

Whatever objectives you decide are appropriate for your operation, they must be **consistent** with other functions and with the strategic objectives of the organisation. Imagine the benefit of everyone talking the same 'objectives language' - the *key objectives template* is just that.

We all care about the customer!

KEY OBJECTIVES TEMPLATE: QSDFC

Do your objectives provide the right template for improving the efficiency of your operation?

Key Objectives Template:

Quality
Speed
Dependability
Flexibility
Cost

These objectives should be customer driven, so **discuss QSDFC with your customers!**
- What do they want? Are they getting it?
- What improvement objectives should you set?

Success in the right QSDFC objectives can give your organisation competitive advantage, and result in happy, loyal customers and increased profits. Let's take a closer look at QSDFC objectives.

Let's all talk the language of QSDFC!

WHAT IS QUALITY?

Doing things right!

You want an interpretation of quality that is objective, not subjective, if you are to drive efficiency improvement. Consider 'error free work' as your quality definition.

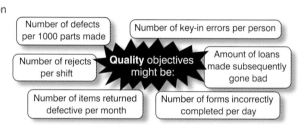

Number of defects per 1000 parts made

Number of key-in errors per person

Number of rejects per shift

Quality objectives might be:

Amount of loans made subsequently gone bad

Number of items returned defective per month

Number of forms incorrectly completed per day

Don't be satisfied with 97% quality, because 3% of your customers are not happy! Motorola aims for six-sigma quality, which is 3.4 defects per million parts manufactured. Other world-class organisations, such as IBM, aim for 'five 9s' – ie: 99.999% right first time.

WHAT IS SPEED?

Doing things fast!

Time is money so we want our processes to flow quickly. We need to measure **how fast things move** in processes.

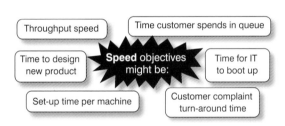

Throughput speed

Time customer spends in queue

Time to design new product

Speed objectives might be:

Time for IT to boot up

Set-up time per machine

Customer complaint turn-around time

Benefits of achieving speed objectives are: minimal delays, faster delivery to customers, faster response to change and reduced work in progress (and therefore less money tied up in working capital).

WHAT IS DEPENDABILITY?

Doing things on time!

Efficiencies are obtained when operations managers can plan ahead. For that they need good forecasting, strong scheduling and reliable processes.

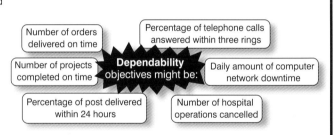

Number of orders delivered on time

Percentage of telephone calls answered within three rings

Number of projects completed on time

Dependability objectives might be:

Daily amount of computer network downtime

Percentage of post delivered within 24 hours

Number of hospital operations cancelled

Benefits of achieving dependability objectives are: less hassle, less 'firefighting', less 'expediting' and greater trust all round, allowing you to plan ahead with more confidence.

WHAT IS FLEXIBILITY?

Adapting to customer requirements!

Nothing stays the same. Customers become more sophisticated, change their minds, new competitors appear, markets decline. The aim should be to **change proactively**, not wait until forced to change by others.

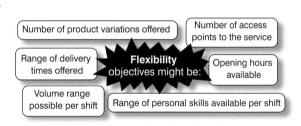

Number of product variations offered

Number of access points to the service

Range of delivery times offered

Flexibility objectives might be:

Opening hours available

Volume range possible per shift

Range of personal skills available per shift

Benefits of achieving flexibility objectives are: being responsive to changes in customer needs, taking quick advantage of market opportunities, being dependable and quick - even during adverse operating conditions.

WHAT IS COST?

The expense of doing business!

Profit = Revenue minus Cost. Activities (and, therefore, processes) generate costs, so eliminating non-value-added activity drives down costs.

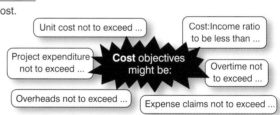

Unit cost not to exceed ...

Cost:Income ratio to be less than ...

Project expenditure not to exceed ...

Cost objectives might be:

Overtime not to exceed ...

Overheads not to exceed ...

Expense claims not to exceed ...

Cost objectives are largely achieved by actions on QSDF.

Benefits are: opportunities to pass more value to the customer, to increase profit margins, to re-invest in resources, to reward staff and investors, etc.

OBJECTIVES VARY

The same mix of QSDFC won't work in every department.
Consider your...

- **Customer and product type:** corporate or personal, wholesale or retail, first class or economy? Understand your customer segment, customer needs for each product, and customer profitability.

- **Work volume and variety:** how much work must your team process? 100,000s or 10s? What variety of work must you process? All products in the range or only one?

- **Competitive position:** is your organisation a market leader or a follower? How do your competitors attract customers? How can you gain advantage?

Let's explore each of these...

SET THE RIGHT OBJECTIVES

CUSTOMER & PRODUCT TYPE

Compare the tyre change service required by a racing driver to that required by a family car driver – a similar product/service but with different customers and needs.

Racing driver's needs:

- **Speed:** car must be returned to the track in minimum time.
- **Quality:** thoroughness of the tyre change is crucial to car's handling at speed. Ultra high quality race tyres expected.
- **Dependability:** *vital that pit crew and tyres perform consistently.*

Family car driver's needs:

- **Cost:** tyre price budgeted for within certain parameters; minimal service fee sought.
- **Flexibility:** ability of garage to provide choice of tyres and prices is important.
- **Quality:** most drivers seek a branded 'good quality' high mileage product - but price must be right.
- **Speed:** minimal wait is important (note success of Kwik Fit).
- **Dependability:** *consistency of garage will determine customer loyalty.*

SET THE RIGHT OBJECTIVES

WORK VOLUME & VARIETY

HIGH volume operations where the variety of work done is low (production lines, back office processing centres, etc.) often define their objectives based upon their process.

Example: large bakeries produce high volumes and have little product variety – they specialise in given product lines, eg: cake.

- **Quality** – you probably have a product specification from your customer; are you meeting it? In high volume processes errors can cause massive disruption. What is your error rate? How do errors affect your operation?
- **Speed** – measures how quickly a batch of products is made. How long does it take to process a unit or batch of your work?
- **Dependability** – means standardisation. Is everything always in place on time so that no part of the process is delayed?
- **Flexibility** – high volume processes are often inflexible to changes in customer demand. They also require a 'critical mass' of work to make high investment in facilities worthwhile. Are you flexible enough? What can you do?
- **Cost** – large customers will demand low costs, so drive unit cost as low as possible but do not compromise quality!

SET THE RIGHT OBJECTIVES

WORK VOLUME & VARIETY

LOW volume operations where the variety of work done is wide (job shops, project teams, craftsmen, specialists) define their objectives based upon customer requirements.

Example: a pharmacist works with relatively low volumes but has to cope with a very wide variety of drugs.

- **Quality** – means whatever the customer values. It may be brand image, price, exclusivity or service; most certainly it involves the customer's perception. Specialist skill sets are important. Do you have them? How can you acquire/develop them?
- **Speed** – is often negotiable; it may depend upon price or product demanded. Efficient work scheduling and workflow are important to keep delays to a minimum. Do you have a work schedule? How well do your processes flow?
- **Dependability** – provided the agreed deadline is met, no one worries. Is anyone complaining about your quality or speed?
- **Flexibility** – every customer is different. How quickly can you adapt to changes?
- **Cost** – how unique is your product/service? Can you charge a premium? Be cost-efficient to maximise the profitability of each transaction.

COMPETITIVE POSITION

Market Leader? Innovative? Original? (eg: Sony)

- Focus on speed – you must be super efficient to be ahead of the game
- Be flexible – constantly think about new products and processes
- Deliver quality – take the risk out of trying something new
- Be dependable – continually delight your customers and reinforce your image
- Control costs – keep the price tempting; don't forget to make a profit!

OR

Market Follower? Risk Averse? (eg: Samsung)

- Focus on cost – your price is critical, so low cost operations are essential
- Be dependable – you must maintain standards to keep costs down
- Maintain speed – react quickly to market leader moves
- Deliver quality – cheap is no excuse for shoddy workmanship
- Avoid excess flexibility – concentrate on your core strengths

 Over time, innovators can stagnate, followers become leaders; how does this impact their objectives?

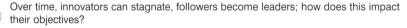

SMART OBJECTIVES DRIVE SUCCESS

Final check: make sure that your objectives are **SMART**, to help you work smarter, not harder, and give you a better chance of achieving efficiency improvement.

Specific — clearly stated and focused on what counts
Measurable — quantified (eg: amount of improvement required)
Agreed — agreement gets buy-in and a higher chance of success
Realistic — get real; set attainable but challenging objectives
Timed — set milestones and deadlines by which the objective is to be achieved

Without clear objectives how would you:

- Know what needs to be done?
- Know how much improvement is required?
- Ensure a collective and motivated effort?
- Know when results are required?

SMART objective example: within three months of project start date, re-work of new business applications to be reduced by 20%.

YOU GET WHAT YOU MEASURE!

A word of warning: the whole point of **SMART** objectives is that they get people or processes to change for the better. Correctly developed and consistently applied, they always succeed in delivering change. So ask yourself:

- 'If we meet or exceed all our objectives, what will actually happen?'
- 'Will the customer be more impressed?'
- 'Will we be more efficient?'
- 'Will we be more profitable?'

If the answer is not 'yes', then why are you wasting your time and effort in achieving non-productive objectives?

Finally, beware of moving goal posts too frequently!

es?

3. Improve work processing
- How can you identify non-value-
  added (wasteful) activity?
- How can you remove it?

HOW EFFICIENT ARE YOUR PROCESSES?

Does work flow smoothly through all stages of your process? Are all steps in the process necessary? Perhaps you suffer from complexity, duplication of effort, errors, re-work, delays, inflexibility, and high costs?

Improving the efficiency of your processes means meeting the needs of three process clients – who will often press for change but will oppose it if it does not meet their needs.

Needs of the three process clients:

1 **Customer needs** = QSDFC (see last section)

2 **Organisation needs** = QSDFC and risks managed through controlled, value-adding processes

3 **Employee needs** = less hassle, motivating jobs, safety and comfort

In this section we will focus on Organisation and Employee needs, and we will introduce an extremely powerful tool (Operations Flow-Charting) that you can quickly use with your people to improve your work processing.

CUSTOMER NEEDS

PRODUCT BENEFITS

Customers buy the benefit(s) that your product or service can give them.

This is all-important. For example, a Toyota car may give benefits of high build QUALITY, DEPENDABLE dealerships, economic running COSTS, etc. These benefits are highly valued by repeat Toyota customers, so Toyota considers them in detail when designing its production and retail processes.

You must ensure you know the benefits **your** customers want. Once you know what they **actually** want (and that is often radically different from what you **think** they want) you can work towards a 'standardised', 'high value-adding' way of processing your work. We'll discuss this more later in this section.

> *'Systems (processes) should be designed to meet the customer's needs rather than the bureaucratic needs of the organisation.'*
>
> Customer Services, Lead Body, UK

IMPROVE WORK PROCESSING

ORGANISATION NEEDS

A solid appreciation of the organisation's needs will not only enable you to decide what must be improved but will also increase your chances of successfully selling your ideas for improvement within the organisation. Needs are often for:

- Planning and control
- Effective controls
- Control through teamwork
- Visible measurement
- Measurements of failure
- Risk management
- Value-added activity
- Elimination of non-value-added activity
- Change control
- Standards
- Good housekeeping

We will now look at each of these in turn.

ORGANISATION NEEDS

PLANNING & CONTROL

Planning looks ahead. Front line managers tend to plan several weeks or a few months ahead. Senior executives typically plan one or two years ahead. Planning ensures resources are used efficiently in meeting objectives.

Control is more immediate. It's done (often by supervisors) here and now with the resources at your disposal. The purpose of control is to ensure that the organisation is effective in achieving its objectives.

If you're failing to plan correctly then you're actually planning future control failures. The result is fire-fighting and, whilst you may still remain effective, you most definitely won't be efficient!

How planning differs from control:

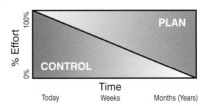

ORGANISATION NEEDS
EFFECTIVE CONTROLS

Effective controls help you to meet your key objectives. They consist of three elements: Measurement, Appraisal and Action.

Think about how a thermostat works in your home...

- **Measurement** – room temperature is measured. This is compared to the desired temperature (the thermostat setting) which is the objective to be met.

- **Appraisal** – calculates the divergence between the actual and desired temperature. Two decision options are considered: to *take action* to alter the temperature (turn the heat up or down) or to *do nothing*. A decision rule may be employed such as 'if actual temp is within 5 degrees of the objective, then do nothing'. The outcome of appraisal is a decision.

- **Action** – implements the decision. Note: doing nothing is only acceptable **if** the objective is being met.

How do your controls ensure that you:
- Process work right?
- Process work on time?
- Process work economically?
- Process work fast?
- Process work when customers change their minds?

IMPROVE WORK PROCESSING

ORGANISATION NEEDS

CONTROL THROUGH TEAMWORK

Are your outputs meeting the needs of your customers? If not, do you need to improve control of your inputs? Or control of your processes? Or both?

You alone will probably not have full control over everything that impacts upon your operations, so seek help and offer help. Control is a team effort. Follow the example of leading companies such as Toyota and Wal-Mart:

- **Visit suppliers** – 'walk through' their process. Do they have the right controls to meet your needs? What can you suggest? How can you encourage them to change?
- **Invite suppliers to visit** – show them how you use their product/service. They may have suggestions for improving your controls/processes, or may take back ideas on how they can give you a better product/service.
- **Invite customers to visit** – show how you make their product/service. Invite their ideas.
- **Visit customers** – how is your product/service used? Can you help each other?

Tip *Always involve your staff. Make regular supplier/customer visits. Take as many of your team as possible – make it a part of their development and your team culture.*

ORGANISATION NEEDS

VISIBLE MEASUREMENT

Measurements are indicators. Clearly visible measurements help to show progress and prompt action (eg: the display on a petrol pump).

The run chart is a straightforward line graph and perhaps the simplest and most powerful way yet to show progress. Use graph paper or a computer spreadsheet package to draw a run chart. The left vertical axis (y) can be used to plot your performance against an objective (eg: the number of items which did not conform to standard) while the bottom horizontal axis (x) can be used to record time periods (eg: hours/days/weeks, etc).

Actual performance can be plotted against any key objective. The most commonly used charts show levels of unsatisfactory *Quality* (eg: errors), *Speed* (eg: excess process time), *Dependability* (eg: number of delays) and *Cost* (eg: excess expenditure).

> **Tip** *Wall-mount run charts for your team; they are a highly useful way to demonstrate where a process is going wrong.*

ORGANISATION NEEDS
MEASUREMENTS OF FAILURE

Do you think that run charts should record the success rate (% of correct items) or the failure rate (% of errors/re-work/delays, etc)?

Many managers feel that it's negative to measure failure. Yet this is what most world-class organisations do! Their reason is that satisfaction with 95%+ success rates often leads to complacency, and complacent companies go backwards, not forwards.

Making failure the focus of measurement prevents this and helps operations to continuously strive to improve performance. This requires a positive improvement culture whereby **errors are seen as opportunities to learn and improve**, not opportunities to blame. Less failure = more success.

> **Tip** *When discussing fail rates with your team, focus on the process not the people. This avoids feelings of persecution and encourages more open discussion. No one goes to work to do a bad job, but bad processes prevent people doing a good job!*

ORGANISATION NEEDS

RISK MANAGEMENT

- **Risk** is an event that could prevent you from meeting your QSDFC objectives.

- **Risk management** involves *risk appraisal* and *contingency planning*.

- **Risk appraisal** is a continuous assessment of both the *likelihood* and *impact* of risks. Understanding how probable a risk is, and the cost to the business if it occurs, allows us to prioritise and helps us to decide whether we need additional or fewer controls.

Risk Impact-Likelihood Matrix

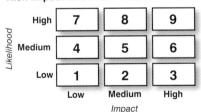

Risks in cell 9 are highest priority, while risks in cell 1 are lowest priority.

ORGANISATION NEEDS

RISK MANAGEMENT

Which risks to your objectives this year score highly on the impact-likelihood matrix? What are your contingency plans?

Contingency planning is planning to cope with the occurrence of a risk (eg: planning to evacuate your employees and switch to backup facilities in the event of fire).

The tragic events and aftermath of September 11th 2001 highlight many issues, not least the threat of terrorism. For example, system interdependencies are greater than ever before: our systems do not exist in isolation to the world; we must consider the effect of system failure within our suppliers and customers.

Exercise *What are the consequences of severe weather upon your operations? Brainstorm the types of risk (eg: water damage to inventory, telephone system failure, air conditioning/heating system failure). Then complete an impact-likelihood matrix and begin to make contingency plans for the most significant events.*

IMPROVE WORK PROCESSING

ORGANISATION NEEDS
SENSIBLY BALANCED CONTROLS

When a risk is identified a common reaction is to add new controls. But, in the wrong place, at the wrong time, they can **slow down** processes, **delay** delivery, **de-motivate** your people, **reduce flexibility**, **increase cost** and so degrade the service given to customers.

Think carefully about the value of each control and, before you implement a control, ask:

- What is the real risk? (See impact-likelihood matrix.)
- What effect will the control have upon our ability to give the customer QSDFC?

Otherwise, you could be handing an opportunity to your competitors to steal your customers by allowing them to provide products and services more simply and less expensively.

Note *Keep your controls under review. A change in circumstances (eg: changed customer needs, changed regulations) may make a control obsolete, counter-productive, or inadequate.*

IMPROVE WORK PROCESSING

ORGANISATION NEEDS

VALUE-ADDED ACTIVITY

Efficient work processing means that value is added at each activity (step) in the process.

Do your activities add value? An activity is either 'value-adding' or is 'non-value-adding' (NVA). NVA activity is wasteful and should be eliminated – customers do not pay for NVA! Two rules of thumb can be applied to test whether an activity adds value or not:

1. **Does the customer value the activity?** If the customer considers what you're doing is important, then the customer is prepared to pay for you to do it. It is, therefore, value-adding activity.

2. **Does the activity get it right first time?** If an error results from an activity then clearly that activity did not add value – it's expensive to rectify mistakes! So, you have to put effort into *getting it right first time*. Such effort reduces waste and adds more value.

ORGANISATION NEEDS

ELIMINATION OF NON-VALUE-ADDING (NVA) ACTIVITY

Operations Flow-Charting (OFC) is the extremely valuable and practical tool we promised you earlier. It is used to identify and challenge NVA and to design more efficient processes. Key features of OFC are:

- **No flow-charting experience or specialist drawing template is required**
- **Classifies activities as 'DO ITS'** – each step of a process is either a **D**elay, **O**peration, **I**nspection, **T**ransportation (any movement) or **S**torage (their flow chart symbols are shown on the next page)
- **Quantifies time taken up** by each step and activity type
- **Quantifies distance involved** in transportation

These features make OFC one of the most user-friendly and powerful process improvement tools. The tool is geared towards identifying non-value-added (NVA) activity and it builds a concise 'finger print' of an operation.

> **Tip** *Before using OFC, clarify the sequence of steps in your process by using Post It™ Notes. Write each step on a single note. Place all the notes on a whiteboard or flip chart and move them around until you're certain you've got the exact order of how things actually happen. You're now ready to prepare your process flow chart.*

ORGANISATION NEEDS

ELIMINATE NON-VALUE-ADDING (NVA) ACTIVITY

OFC activity symbols – 'DO ITS'

 Delay (eg: waiting, queuing)

 Operation (eg: doing the work that **must** be done)

 Inspection (eg: checking the work)

 Transportation (eg: moving the work from one location to another - even across an office)

 Storage (eg: placed in stock, filed in cabinet)

IMPROVE WORK PROCESSING

ORGANISATION NEEDS

ELIMINATE NON-VALUE-ADDING (NVA) ACTIVITY

Using the OFC. Consider yourself as the 'work' passing through the process. Eg: in a complaint handling process, consider yourself as the 'complaint'. Observe the process and chart every step as it actually occurs, **not** how it's meant to occur.

Deciding on the type of activity. At each step in the process, ask what is happening to the work. Using the example above, ask: 'Am I the *complaint* ...

- Waiting around, while something else is happening – a **D**elay
- Being changed or used to create something – an **O**peration
- Being reviewed/checked – an **I**nspection
- Being moved – a **T**ransportation
- Being filed/archived – a **S**torage

See worked example on next page. Each step is numbered and briefly described. The activity type is selected and the length of time taken to complete it is recorded. If the activity is a transportation, distance is recorded. An arrow is drawn from the previous type of activity to the current one, illustrating the flow of work through each activity. Finally, each page of OFC is totalled up and, when the full process has been charted, all pages are totalled. Thus, you can quantify NVA and hence justify improvements.

46

ORGANISATION NEEDS

ELIMINATE NON-VALUE-ADDING (NVA) ACTIVITY

OFC – example

Processing a new business application (app.):

Step	Description	Activity Type					Time	Dist
1	Wait for app.	▷	○	▢	⇒	▽	10 mins	–
2	Take app. to desk	▷	○	▢	⇒	▽	2 mins	15 m
3	Date stamp app.	▷	○	▢	⇒	▽	5 secs	–
4	Check app. completion	▷	○	▢	⇒	▽	5 mins	–
5	Wait while input	▷	○	▢	⇒	▽	6 m 15 s	–
6	Wait until a/c updated	▷	○	▢	⇒	▽	7 secs	–
7	Check app. to screen	▷	○	▢	⇒	▽	2 m 19 s	–
8	Move to filing cabinet	▷	○	▢	⇒	▽	1 m 11 s	5 m
9	Wait	▷	○	▢	⇒	▽	15 mins	–
10	File app.	▷	○	▢	⇒	▽	6 secs	–
	TOTALS	**4**	**1**	**2**	**2**	**1**	**42 m 3 s**	**20 m**

ORGANISATION NEEDS

ELIMINATE NON-VALUE-ADDING (NVA) ACTIVITY

To improve the process using OFC, ask the following questions:

- **How can we eliminate Delays?** (Can we receive applications earlier? Should we start work later? Can we input applications faster? Can the computer be updated faster?)
- **Are all Operations necessary? Can some be combined/eliminated?** (Is it vital to date-stamp applications?)
- **Are all Inspections necessary? Can some be eliminated?** (Do our checks reveal errors? Can we eliminate the root cause [see p 93] perhaps through training? Should we alter the application or computer screen?
- **Are all Transportations necessary? Can we reduce the distance involved?** (Can we alter the office layout to reduce distance and save time? Make the layout work efficiently for your process.)
- **Are all Storages necessary? What do we keep for too long?** (Is there a better alternative to filing the application? Consider other options, eg: scanning, while recognising legal requirements.)

Challenge every activity and the order in which activities are done. Often, over 75% of all processing time can be eliminated this way!

IMPROVE WORK PROCESSING

ORGANISATION NEEDS

CHANGE CONTROL

Warning - beware of uncontrolled process change!

Uncontrolled change poses a huge risk to standardisation. Therefore, before implementing process change, involve your line manager and find out about any *change control* process to which proposals should be submitted.

- **Change control** processes authorise, co-ordinate and maximise the value of change for all process stakeholders. In brief, change control helps to maintain *process uniformity.*

- **Process uniformity** means performing repetitive tasks in the same way – the 'standard way'. It applies to geographically distinct operations performing the same tasks and also to individuals involved with the same task.

We maintain and improve process uniformity so that we can provide a consistent service to customers. Standards are critically important in this process.

IMPROVE WORK PROCESSING

ORGANISATION NEEDS
STANDARDS

> **25%**
> *of all errors made are caused by poor standards*

Source:
'Gemba Kaizen', by
Masaaki Imai, 1997, McGraw-Hill

50

ORGANISATION NEEDS

STANDARDS

- Standards are known by many different names, including *policies, operating procedures* and *specifications*.

- Standards should state SMART performance dimensions for the product or service being delivered and also for the process or environment delivering it. They should steer work processes towards achievement of QSDFC.

- Standards embody and preserve our knowledge of how work should be done.

- Don't leave your standards to gather dust in your bottom drawer! Take them out of your drawer and breathe new life into them by making sure they match up to the following checklist.

IMPROVE WORK PROCESSING

ORGANISATION NEEDS

STANDARDS' CHECKLIST

Your standards should:

- Represent the best, easiest and safest way to do a job
- Offer the best way to preserve know-how and expertise
- Provide a way to measure performance
- Show the relationship between cause and effect
- Provide a basis for both maintenance and improvement
- Provide objectives and indicate training goals
- Provide a basis for training
- Provide a basis for audit or diagnosis
- Create a basis for preventing recurrence of errors and minimising variability
- Provide a means for preventing recurrence of errors and minimising variability

Source:
'Gemba Kaizen',
by Masaaki Imai,
1997, McGraw-Hill

IMPROVE WORK PROCESSING

ORGANISATION NEEDS

GOOD HOUSEKEEPING

Poor housekeeping causes 50% of all errors made.

Masaaki Imai, a Japanese industrial improvement expert, recommends a '5S' approach to good housekeeping:

Sort   out what is necessary (what you really need to do the job) from what is unnecessary (those things that have accumulated over the years).

Straighten   out the workplace. Make sure everything has a place and everything is kept in place.

Scrub   the workplace. Keep the work site tidy at all times.

Standardise   Establish standards for housekeeping and stick to them!

Systematise   Make the activities above part of your team discipline and culture; something you do every day without fail.

ORGANISATION NEEDS
GOOD HOUSEKEEPING

Housekeeping is not just mops and buckets! It relates to your attention to many aspects of the workplace and systems.

Consider how your customers would rate your standards of:

- Database maintenance
- Filing accuracy and retrieval
- Organisation of storage systems
- Material handling
- Workplace cleaning
- Staff appearance
- Watering of office plants

If you think that customers would not be satisfied with your standards, then why should you be satisfied?

IMPROVE WORK PROCESSING

EMPLOYEE NEEDS
WELL-DESIGNED JOBS

People make processes work. So, although you need to maximise your process to achieve success in QSDFC, you may have to curtail some of your plans to reflect the needs of the people who will work the process. Good people are increasingly difficult to find, therefore it is vital to succeed at attracting them and then keeping them in your process. For that you need good job design.

- Good job design underpins successful work processing by guiding and motivating people to meet and, even, exceed their performance objectives.

- Job design and process design must be considered together. Attention to job design issues is vital if the full capacity of a process is to be achieved.

- People strive to make a process happen within an environment that is motivational and safe.

Effective job design can deliver more for less. In the new millennium it still draws upon several 20th century developments, which we will now examine, namely:
job simplification, ergonomics, behaviourism, and **empowerment.**

EMPLOYEE NEEDS
JOB SIMPLIFICATION

This involves breaking jobs down into many separate, simple tasks so that one person does one task many times over and very quickly (classic production line). Complex products/services can be assembled in high volumes (eg: car manufacture). It delivers speed and volume, but how well does it deliver quality, flexibility and reliability?

Nowadays, machines and computers do simple tasks quickly, reliably and with few errors but they are often expensive and inflexible. Why then is the production line still a valid process?

- Jobs (ie: people) are easy to measure, to set targets for, to **control**
- People can be quickly trained to do simple tasks
- Highly skilled people aren't needed, so wages are low
- Jobs are easily automated, allowing for further efficiencies
- Production can easily be moved to new locations if wages rise or workers become scarce
- Some employees may not want, or be capable of, more varied work

But the problem is, people often don't like production lines (the work is boring!)
Over simplification often leads to high absenteeism/staff turnover, high costs from errors and slowness to react to change. What to do?

IMPROVE WORK PROCESSING

EMPLOYEE NEEDS

ERGONOMICS

Ergonomics attempts to 'fit the work environment to people' not 'fit people to the work environment'. Simple examples of ergonomics in action are: desks altered to be at the right height for the individual user, frequently used tools re-positioned to be close at hand, and VDUs positioned at the right angle to minimise eye and neck strain.

The result is a healthier, safer and more productive work environment, allowing you to get more for less: more production because there is less strain (ie: wasted effort) in performing jobs and less cost because absenteeism drops and staff turnover goes down. Attention to ergonomic detail often entails investment in layout and materials and is heavily driven by health and safety legislation. Badly designed jobs can have the potential to injure people who do the same repetitive actions and motions, day in day out. Today, 'repetitive strain injury' or RSI is a widely recognised problem.

- What ergonomic improvements to your workplace have you seen in the last few years?
- How have these helped to improve your work processing?
- What future improvements are planned?
- How will these further help to improve your work processing?

You've now got people working faster by paying attention to ergonomics, what next?

IMPROVE WORK PROCESSING

EMPLOYEE NEEDS

BEHAVIOURISM: JOB ENRICHMENT

You can reduce boredom in simplified jobs by rotating staff frequently between jobs. However, staff quickly recognise that now they do several boring jobs. Ergonomics reduces stress, strain and injury risk but to really move forward, you have to understand what people get from work. Designing the following characteristics into jobs can improve job satisfaction and the efficiency of people in processes.

1. Task Identity (What am I doing?)	• How clear and meaningful is the task? • Does the task have obvious start and finish points?
2. Task Significance (Why am I doing it?)	• How important is the task? • What effect does it have on others? (eg: contribution that the job makes to achievement of QSDFC)
3. Task Variety (Let me feel I'm skilled)	• How much of a challenge is the task? • Does the task require a range of skills?
4. Autonomy (Let me feel in control)	• How much discretion does the individual have in performing his/her tasks? (eg: timing, sequencing, choice of methods/tools, etc)
5. Feedback (Show me respect and make me feel valued)	• How much information is given to the individual about how well the task has been performed?

Adapted from: J.R. Hackman et al, 'A New Strategy For Job Enrichment', California Management Review, 1975, Vol 17, No 3

A job scoring high on each of these characteristics is **enriched** and one that people will want to do. However, to enrich a job you may well have to redesign the process.

EMPLOYEE NEEDS
EMPLOYMENT

EMPOWERMENT

Empowerment (from the 1980s/90s)

The ultimate attempt to allow staff to feel they can influence their own work (and, therefore, achieve satisfaction) is currently empowerment. It majors on **autonomy** by increasing the authority of staff to take decisions that previously would have been taken by managers. For example, leading car rental groups and hotels now empower their check-in staff to give appropriate up-grades when the car or room type required is unavailable or to make refunds to unhappy customers – all without reference to a manager.

Empowerment can, therefore, improve response times and service recovery. Generally, it encourages staff to take more initiative, which is good in today's rapidly changing work environment. However, it can be threatening for 'traditional' managers. It is also not an opportunity for management to 'hand over responsibility' to workers. It must be supported by the correct management style, appropriate training, clear performance objectives, constant feedback and well-defined limits of discretionary behaviour. Most definitely empowerment is not an opportunity for abdication of management accountability and it will not work in 'blame' cultures.

EMPLOYEE NEEDS

EMPOWERMENT: MANAGEMENT CHALLENGES

Are you empowering your people? Have you:

- Positioned customer satisfaction as the No.1 goal of the business?
- Defined SMART performance objectives?
- Defined boundaries of acceptable behaviour and decision-making?
- Established an open and honest relationship with your people, boss and peer group?
- Motivated your people? What carrots are you using?
- Established a management style like that of a tutor, a facilitator, a mentor?
- Provided appropriate training programmes?
- Held regular performance meetings with your people?

If not, then why? What can you do to improve? If some of these factors are outside your ability to control or influence, then maybe empowerment is inappropriate.

systematic approach
to constant improvement?

3.

4. Increase capacity
- Are you meeting demand?
- What action(s) can you take?
- How efficient are your resources?

WHAT IS CAPACITY?

> *Capacity is the maximum achievable output over a period of time, given a known level of available resources**

*Resources = people, materials, information, facilities

To ensure that customer needs for QSDFC are met **profitably**, your processes must have sufficient capacity to meet customer demand.

INCREASE CAPACITY

BEGIN WITH FORECASTING DEMAND

Forecasting demand allows you to plan the right levels of resources to process your workloads.

Forecasting Demand

Remember, the further ahead you forecast the greater the potential for error.

Identify patterns: peaks, troughs, annually, monthly, weekly, hourly.

Planning

Consider **5Ws** and **3Hs**:
• What, When, Why, Where, Who
• How, How much £, How many

You need to have a sound understanding of the demand for your service or product. Effective forecasting can provide that understanding.

Note *Failing to forecast is failing to plan! And failing to plan is planning to fail! Let's take a look at some ways to forecast…*

INCREASE CAPACITY

WAYS TO FORECAST

- **Moving averages**
  (eg: the average demand for our product each day, based upon an average over the last three days, is…)

- **Mathematical (regression) models**
  (eg: if Marketing increase their spend by 10%, demand will rise by 6%…)

- **Intuition**
  (eg: 'My gut feeling is…')

- **Expert opinion**
  (eg: industry analysts expect demand for your product to grow by x% in the next six months)

MOVING AVERAGES

This is the simplest and, yet, one of the most effective methods of forecasting demand. Demand for the next period (eg: hour/day/week) is forecast by averaging demand over a specified number of previous periods. For example, a manufacturer of an air conditioning unit uses the last six weeks' sales figures to forecast demand:

Week 31	Week 32	Week 33	Week 34	Week 35	Week 36	Week 37
135	123	140	137	115	116	?

Forecast demand (moving average) for wk 37 = $\frac{(135+123+140+137+115+116)}{6}$ = **128**

If actual demand for wk 37 turned out to be 126, what would your forecast be for wk 38? Tip: total up the actuals for the previous six weeks (wks 32-7) and divide by 6 – simple! Note we've moved forward by one week – hence 'moving average'.

Examples *Clothing retailers use a six-week moving average to forecast weekly sales; and telephone banking call centres forecast call volumes in the next half hour by looking at the moving average for the day and half hour in question over the last four weeks.*

ALTERNATIVE FORECASTING OPTIONS

Simple averages of demand will be sufficient for most line operations, but sometimes something else is required.

Regression models – Useful for more complicated relationships where multiple influences have to be factored in. Unless you like statistics, leave it to the experts. However, if they can't explain their model to you in plain English, do you want to trust it?

Intuition – Are you psychic? Most of us aren't, so be wary. However, with skilled people it can work and may be necessary when introducing a new process (no one has ever done it before so no records exist to analyse).

Expert opinion – Experience counts for a lot. But, no market stays the same for long so it can be dangerous to rely on just one expert. Invite opinions from many, listen to the 'heretics' and look outside the company for some advice. Too many companies get their plans wrong because they looked inwards, listened only to 'comforting' advice and ignored the real danger signals.

INCREASE CAPACITY

FORECASTING: ASKING 'WHAT IF?'

Constantly look ahead – plan for 'what if?' scenarios.

Whichever way you forecast demand you may have to adjust your forecast according to your expectations about future circumstances. What scenarios (events and conditions) are likely in the forecast period?

- Be aware of the main factors that affect demand for your service (eg: marketing campaigns, events, interest rates, time of year, daily and hourly patterns, the weather, etc)

- Review likely scenarios by asking 'what if?'

Review your demand forecasts for the next six months – ask 'what if?'.

What if a quarter-end and a month-end coincide on the day before a major public holiday? Such an event was always likely to create peak transaction demand for BACS (the UK's inter-bank payment system) but BACS failed to ensure that their system had enough capacity to cope with this event in 1997. The result was a system crash, several million unhappy customers and a major embarrassment to the banks!

LONG-TERM CAPACITY PLANNING OPTIONS

Operations should choose a **capacity planning option (or strategy)** that is best suited to their own demand pattern over the long-term (typically the next two years).

3 Capacity Planning Options:

level   Or   chase   Or   mixed

The aim is to maximise profitability by maximising productivity and minimising resource wastage. This requires high levels of resource **utilisation** and **efficiency**, which we will discuss later in this section. First, let's look at the implications of each of these options...

LONG-TERM CAPACITY PLANNING OPTIONS

LEVEL – A fixed level of capacity is used to meet demand.
Examples: operating theatres, fire service, some large bakeries, mining.
For: keeps output constant; ignores demand fluctuation.
Against: excess resources/stock in off-peak periods; stock shortages during peaks.

CHASE – Capacity continuously altered to meet demand. The only choice is whether to alter capacity before or after demand changes.
Examples: supermarkets, leisure attractions, call centres.
For: changes resources to meet forecast demand.
Against: many adjustments; need to react quickly to demand changes; hard to maintain consistent quality.

MIXED – A combination of the above two: **level** in flat demand periods, **chase** in peaks/troughs. Pressure within most operations to reduce cost while meeting customer needs for QSDF often leads to this 'mixed' approach.
Most operations apply this approach. Some are moving from a level to a mixed approach by using schemes such as 'annualised hours' to better fit their manpower to demand.
For: combines advantages of level and chase, hence tends to be less costly.
Against: more adjustments than level; imbalance between resources/demand at peaks/troughs.

CAPACITY RISKS

Every day you face these risks:

Too little capacity:
- Overworked
- Shortcuts
- Overtime
- Sickness
- Machine breakdowns

Too much capacity:
- Boredom
- Complacency
- Absenteeism
- Poor maintenance

Risks can lead to:
- Reduced quality
- Delays
- Missed deadlines
- Reduced flexibility

Resulting in:
- Lost customers
- Reduced revenue
- Increased costs
- Reduced profits

AVOIDING CAPACITY RISKS

Did you recognise any of the capacity risks in your own operation?

Even after well-researched capacity planning decisions, managers are faced with a continuous challenge: too little or too much capacity (ie: too few or too many resources) to meet fluctuating customer demand.

There are three broad options to attempt to balance our resources with demand, and hence avoid or minimise capacity risks:

1. Change demand, or
2. Change resources, or
3. Change both demand and resources

AVOIDING CAPACITY RISKS
CHANGE DEMAND

Changing demand is often ignored by managers and considered a 'marketing problem' - **it's not!** It's an operations problem too! Consider:

- **Segmenting demand** (eg: by customer types, product types) and take only the most profitable demand – ignore the rest

- **Offering price incentives** (eg: 'two for one') and stimulate sales

- **Promoting off-peak demand** (eg: 'half price before 11 a.m.') and move demand to slack periods

- **Using queuing systems** (eg: appointment/reservation systems) and have customers wait

- **Developing complimentary services** (eg: airline 'executive lounges') and offer alternative services or goods in off peak periods

AVOIDING CAPACITY RISKS
CHANGE RESOURCES

Better management of resources can increase your capacity. Consider:

- **Overtime** (the most common approach) - work staff longer

- **Increase customer participation** in the process – get them to do more work, but you may have to educate and incentivise

- **Cross-training or 'multi-skilling' staff** – share skills in peak periods

- **Work shifts** – move resources to peak periods

- **Part-time (or temporary) employees**

- **Annualised hours** – mirror trends over the year

- **Sharing and borrowing capacity** – work with other managers to spread the load

MEASURING CAPACITY

Do you know how much work your people and machines are capable of?

Do you know how efficient your people and machines are?

You probably have some idea, maybe based upon experience.

Without a reasonable expectation of what your resources are capable of, your planning and work allocation are highly suspect, and you cannot judge whether you are using your resources efficiently.

Machine design capacity is often stamped on the machine or recorded in the instruction book. You get no such luxury with people – you have to measure their work and work it out yourself!

Capacity measures form the basis of capacity control and help us to decide how to adjust our capacity. The key capacity measures are given on the next page.

KEY CAPACITY CONTROL MEASURES

Design capacity   A theoretical ideal level of output *assuming no stoppages* – whether *planned or **unplanned.

Effective capacity   The maximum output that can be achieved in a specified time based on a known level of available resources and taking *planned* stoppages into account.

Utilisation   Actual output divided by design capacity – expressed as a %. Measures the level of design capacity used.

Efficiency   Actual output divided by effective capacity – expressed as a %.

Productivity   A rate of output in relation to a measure of resource used (eg: ten widgets per man-hour).

*Planned stoppages   = unavoidable losses of time (eg: training, maintenance, regular team meetings)

**Unplanned stoppages   = avoidable losses of time (eg: sickness, downtime, and interruptions)

CAPACITY CONTROL & WORK MEASUREMENT

Before we can measure efficiency or utilisation, etc, we must know what our resources are capable of.

Work measurement is:
the application of techniques to find the time for a
qualified operator to carry out a specific job
at a defined level of performance.

(International Labour Organisation)

The aim is to find the **standard time** to do a job. Knowledge of how much one person (or team) can do in a period of time underpins all labour capacity calculations.

CALCULATING STANDARD TIME

The standard time calculation takes 'basic time' (the average of many timed observations of a specific task at a judged rate of performance – eg: 85% out of 100%) and adds an allowance for fatigue (eg: 12%).

Note: judgements about ratings are best performed by qualified work study experts. Ratings can, however, be automated. For example, bar code scanners and computers in supermarkets allow a standard to be set for transaction processing at tills, against which the performance of operators is measured.

Example: calculating standard time to input 'form F':

Observation:	1	2	3	4	5	6	7	8	9	10	Ave
Observed Time	2.20	2.25	2.24	2.11	2.00	2.21	2.09	1.99	2.17	2.29	**2.16**
Rating %	80%	80%	80%	85%	90%	80%	85%	90%	80%	90%	
Basic Time	1.76	1.80	1.79	1.79	1.80	1.77	1.78	1.79	1.74	2.06	**1.81**

Standard Time = Basic Time plus Allowance for Fatigue = 1.81 x 1.12 = 2.03 mins

A qualified and motivated person would be expected to input one 'form F' every 2.03 minutes or 29 per hour (60 / 2.03). Assuming a 7.5hr working day, the daily capacity is 217 (i.e. 7.5hrs x 29 per hr).

CAPACITY CONTROL CALCULATIONS

Worked example:

A data input team of three people is responsible for the input of *form F*. At 8.30 am yesterday its outstanding workload was 700 forms. By the end of the 7.5hr workday the team had input 460 forms. During the day the computer system unexpectedly crashed for 1hr and the team attended a planned meeting with its manager for half an hour. One of the team took a half-day of planned holiday.

Design capacity = 29 per hr x 7.5hrs x 3 workers = <u>652</u>
Effective capacity = 29 per hr x (7.5 – 0.5hr) x 2.5 workers = <u>507</u>
Utilisation = 460/652 = <u>71%</u>
Efficiency = 460/507 = <u>91%</u>
Productivity (per hr worked) = 460/(7hrs x 2.5 workers) = 25.9

Note *This is a simple demonstration of the link between work measurement and capacity measurement. Some work measurement systems make this more complex by including contingency for stoppages in their 'allowances', and hence increase standard times. Please also note that if you change the way someone performs a task then the standard time should be re-calculated. This subject is complex and not to be taken lightly!*

ESTABLISH TARGETS

Capacity measures give you a basis for adjusting your resources in order to increase efficiency, etc. But what targets should be set and what are the danger signs?

Efficiency: aim for 100%. You should be working to drive all unplanned stoppages out of your operation.

Utilisation: unlike efficiency, we cannot suggest a target that would be suitable for all operations. Consider the utilisation of airline check-in operations. Checking in economy customers on a trans-Atlantic flight during the summer has very high utilisation – long queues and delays go hand in hand with this. Contrast this to the lower utilisation of check-in operators dealing with first class passengers, who expect short queues and attentive service.

Generally, over time utilisation rises. Finance managers often push for 100% but seasoned operations managers resist strongly. Why?

INCREASE CAPACITY

ESTABLISH TARGETS

Watch out for the following **danger signs!**

Low utilisation (consistently less than 75%)
- Is the operation over capacity?
- Do customers perceive low quality?
- You have excess costs in the process.
- Consider improving staff training, increasing demand or redesigning the process.

High utilisation (consistently more than 90%)
- Is the operation under capacity?
- Do customers receive inferior service levels?
- You have excess costs from delays; frustration; risk of injury; re-work.
- Consider decreasing demand, streamlining processes.

- How effective have your
  efforts been?
- How can you tell?

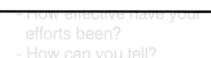

5. Continuously improve
- Do you have a
  systematic approach
  to constant improvement?

4. Increase capacity
- Are you meeting demand?
- What action(s) can you take?

CONTINUOUSLY IMPROVE

STANDING STILL IS *NOT* AN OPTION!

Your operation must adapt and improve **continuously.** Why?

- New competitors arrive all the time
- New products arrive daily
- Customers become more demanding
- Costs must go down, revenue up
- Increasing pressure for more with less
- Increasing automation and use of IT

All this means rapid change!

HOW MUCH IMPROVEMENT?

Large, one-off investments to up-grade people, machinery, computers, etc, often fail to give sustainable performance improvement.

Without management commitment to a continuous incremental improvement culture, cost savings are usually short-lived and costs tend to creep back up!

You may have the best computer systems, manufacturing plant, etc, in your industry **but** don't be complacent. Preserve the advantage of these investments by committing to continuous improvement.

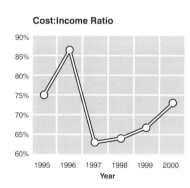

Cost:Income Ratio

CONTINUOUSLY IMPROVE

WHY INCREMENTAL CHANGE?

World-class organisations such as Sony and Motorola apply an incremental approach to improvement. Their managers know the value of many small, low-cost, improvement steps implemented continuously. They **involve their people**, as the best ideas for continuous improvement come from the people who actually do the work. Improvement is systematic and preventative.

Incremental change is non-threatening, non-confrontational, often cheap to implement, easy to manage and, above all, allows everyone to contribute.

Many small steps	✔
Low cost	✔
Simple to maintain	✔

BE SYSTEMATIC

There is no point improving a process unless that improvement is valued by the customer or by the business.

Provided you can satisfactorily ensure that this is the case, you should then progress **systematically** through four stages: **P-D-C-A**.

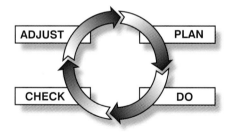

DECIDE WHAT YOU WANT

Before setting out on improvement ask your team: **'What are we trying to achieve and why?'**

- What needs improving?
- Can a quick fix be put in place? (temporary solution only)
- What is the root cause of the problem? (see root cause analysis, p 93)
- What options are there for corrective action?
- What action(s) are we going to take?
- What are our objectives?
- How will we implement our chosen action(s)?

Don't 'DO' without a PLAN!

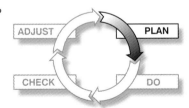

IMPLEMENT SUCCESSFULLY

Careful thought needs to be given to how to implement any improvement. Here are three major options:

Big Bang - if change has to happen all at once. This may require a lot of resources if the improvement is significant and is a high-risk strategy, so have a contingency plan!

Pilot/Trial - trial locations/wearer trials/pilot schemes/pilot systems, etc, allow you to learn from real experience and improve before final implementation.

Phased Roll Out - if the change affects many locations or areas of the business then a staggered or phased approach may be best. This makes good use of constrained resources, allowing an improvement task force team to implement a standard solution one location at a time. Pilot schemes usefully precede this approach.

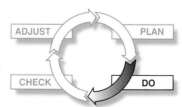

CONTINUOUSLY IMPROVE

CHECK PERFORMANCE

Check actual performance against the objectives set. Investigate any divergence.

Note, our plan should have specified:

- What to measure and why
- What measurement technique
- How to record and analyse
- When to measure
- Where to measure
- Who is going to measure
- Who needs feedback and when
- How results should be presented

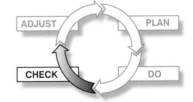

CONTINUOUSLY IMPROVE

LOCK IN IMPROVEMENTS

Did the improvement achieve the desired results?

- If yes, lock in your improvement – make it your new standard.

  What now needs to be achieved and why? Select the next improvement issue and go through the P-D-C-A cycle.

- If no, what have you learned about the problem? Use this knowledge to decide what further adjustments are necessary to meet the objectives. Begin a new P-D-C-A cycle – continuously improve.

*Don't forget: some problems
take many cycles of P-D-C-A,
so celebrate and reward sustained
effort as well as quick results!*

CONTINUOUSLY IMPROVE

KAIZEN

In Japan, continuous improvement is known as *Kaizen*.

Kaizen describes the management practices of leading Japanese businesses and is now applied by many world-class organisations. Masaaki Imai, a Japanese management consultant, introduced these concepts to western managers in the late 1980s.

Kaizen encourages managers and their people to work together to:

- Solve problems at their source
- Maintain and improve standards
- Improve housekeeping
- Eliminate waste

'Kaizen means continuous improvement in personal life, home life, social life, and working life as a whole. As related to the workplace, kaizen means continuing improvement involving managers and workers, customers and suppliers alike.'

NASA, Langley Research Center

See the earlier chapter entitled 'Improve Work Processing'.

CONTINUOUSLY IMPROVE

GO TO GEMBA!

Kaizen says: Got a problem? Go to Gemba!

Gemba is where work is done. Many managers still spend woefully little time outside their offices. Even in today's open plan environments many remain glued to their desks. Why?! Perhaps they think that only a major investment will solve their problems or that the answers lie elsewhere – in Finance, Marketing or Computing departments. Ironically, most answers lie close by; at Gemba, where the work is being done!

Going to Gemba forces management and staff to work **together**, at the **place where the error is occurring**. Attempting to resolve problems in isolation (perhaps in a management meeting) without visiting the workplace and involving the people who actually do the work is a recipe for failure.

- If the problem is computer input errors, go to the input area
- If the problem is high levels of scrap, go to the production area

CONTINUOUSLY IMPROVE

ELIMINATE WASTE

Where to look for waste:

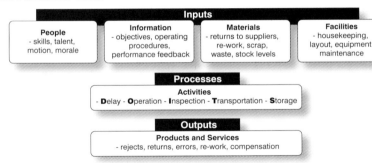

Inputs

People	**Information**	**Materials**	**Facilities**
- skills, talent, motion, morale	- objectives, operating procedures, performance feedback	- returns to suppliers, re-work, scrap, waste, stock levels	- housekeeping, layout, equipment maintenance

Processes

Activities
- **D**elay - **O**peration - **I**nspection - **T**ransportation - **S**torage

Outputs

Products and Services
- rejects, returns, errors, re-work, compensation

You should produce exactly what the customer wants, efficiently and economically - no more, no less.

ROOT CAUSE ANALYSIS

It's no use treating symptoms, you must find the root causes of problems and eliminate them. A simple but highly effective technique to use with your people is:

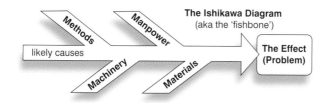

The Ishikawa Diagram
(aka the 'fishbone')

In the 'head' of the fish, name the problem you are analysing. Brainstorm each 'M' with your team to find likely root causes: from each 'M' draw and label bones for causes, then brainstorm these causes to find their root causes – again draw and label bones from each of them. Note you may have to ask the question 'Why' five times or more before you get to the real roots of the problem.

CONTINUOUSLY IMPROVE

12 STEPS TO CONTINUOUS IMPROVEMENT

Here is Hewlett-Packard's 12-step approach:

1	Select the quality issue	
2	Write an issue statement	
3	Identify the process	
4	Draw a flow chart	
5	Select a process performance measure	**Plan**
6	Conduct a cause and effect analysis	
7	Collect and analyse data	
8	Identify major causes of the quality issue	
9	Plan for improvements	
10	Take corrective action	**Do**
11	Are the objectives met?	**Check**
12	If yes, document and standardise changes	**Adjust**

Adapted and used with permission of Hewlett-Packard.

6. Check customer perception
- How effective have your efforts been?
- How can you tell?

5. Continuously improve
- Do you have a
systematic approach

95

CUSTOMER SURVEYS

Improving efficiency should bring about greater customer satisfaction. This is measured through customer surveys. Their sole purpose is to acquire a most valuable asset – customer feedback.

- Customers can teach us a lot about our service and our product.

- If we're not willing to learn from our customers then you can bet that our competitors are!

Since customer surveys require time, effort and cost on the parts of both the organisation and the customer, their design is all-important.

WHO SHOULD YOU LISTEN TO?

**Managers'
perceptions vs
customers' perceptions.**

Improving Efficiency

Health Warning!

Questioning customer feedback or
looking for excuses can be seriously
damaging to your results.

The customer's perception is their reality and all that matters.

Open and honest analysis helps us to better understand our customers and our operations. Marketing and Operations Managers: ignore this at your peril!

THE FAILURE OF TRADITIONAL CUSTOMER SURVEYS

Unfortunately, most surveys cling to a traditional style of asking customers whether something did or did not work and whether they liked or disliked something. This does not provide us with the detail required for improving our processes.

Pitfalls in survey design – **some don'ts:**

Don't ignore factors that colour customer perceptions

Don't ignore the process that the customer actually experienced

Don't ignore specific incidents, good and bad, that the customer experienced

Don't use narrow rating/scoring scales of 1 to 3

Don't use 'smiley' faces

ANALYSING CUSTOMER SURVEYS

Analysis of data is often pre-occupied with categorising the socio-demographic features of respondents (eg: age, income, etc) and looking for correlation with factors such as the weather. These factors do, of course, influence the customer's buying behaviour, but the customer's **experience** of the product or service is critical to your improvement effort.

Lies, damn lies and statistics!

- Beware of averages – if you gear improvement to averages, guess what sort of improvement you'll get? Yes, average!

- There is no such thing as an average customer!

- Beware of analysis paralysis!

- Don't waste effort trying to rationalise poor results!

- Be honest – share the results.

- So, some customers feel better on sunny days. How does that help us to improve efficiency?

CHECK CUSTOMER PERCEPTION

FOUR SURVEY TOOLS

Four important recent developments are:

1. Critical Incident Technique
2. Importance-Performance
3. Customer Processing Framework
4. Determinants of Service Quality

The aim of each approach is to capture information which managers can use to take appropriate action to improve processes and service delivery.

CRITICAL INCIDENT TECHNIQUE (CIT)

After asking your customers to rate aspects of your service, ask them to describe 'critical incidents' or, in other words, what was especially good and what was especially bad. For example:

Describe two extremely good things about the service

Describe two terrible things about the service

Concise design of questionnaires is vital, and CIT helps to ensure that you don't miss out things that the customer feels are critically important. This helps you to prioritise action and to identify and learn from 'pockets of excellence' within your operation or other parts of the organisation.

Remember to leave enough blank space for meaningful responses!

CHECK CUSTOMER PERCEPTION

IMPORTANCE-PERFORMANCE

Finding out the importance, as well as the performance, of what you do compared with your competitors provides a solid base for prioritising improvement.

Most survey questionnaires ask the customer to rate the **performance** of aspects of the service.

Please rate the user manual

But if we don't ask customers how **important** these aspects are...

How important is the user manual?

- How do we know that our efforts are spent on the right things? And...
- How can we prioritise improvement?

IMPORTANCE-PERFORMANCE MATRIX

Using a rating scale of 1 to 9 (see definitions over page) researchers have developed the following 4-zone matrix which aids prioritisation:

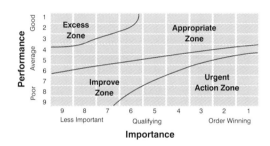

The 4 zones:

If many customers rate the performance of a feature highly, but rate its importance as very low, we are being excessive in our service provision (ie: in the **excess** zone). We should consider using the resources dedicated to supporting this feature elsewhere - for example, to improve an important feature with a low performance (ie: in the **urgent action** zone).

Source: Slack et al, Operations Management 4th Ed, 2003.
Reprinted with permission of Pearson Education Ltd.

CHECK CUSTOMER PERCEPTION

IMPORTANCE-PERFORMANCE RATINGS

	Score	Interpretation	
Importance	1.	Provides crucial advantage	Order Winners
	2.	Provides important advantage	
	3.	Provides useful advantage	
	4.	Must be top standard	Order Qualifiers
	5.	Must be average standard	
	6.	Must be close to average	
	7.	Not currently important	Less Important
	8.	Unlikely to be important	
	9.	Not considered	
Performance	1.	Consistently much better than our closest rival	Is Better
	2.	Consistently better than our closest rival	
	3.	Consistently marginally better than our closest rival	
	4.	Often marginally better than most	Is Average
	5.	Same as the others	
	6.	Often close to the others	
	7.	Usually worse than some	Is Worse
	8.	Often worse than most	
	9.	Consistently the worst	

Source: Slack et al, Operations Management 4th Ed, 2003.
Reprinted with permission of Pearson Education Ltd.

CHECK CUSTOMER PERCEPTION

CUSTOMER PROCESSING FRAMEWORK

Here is a seven-stage framework used to examine customers' service experience as they pass through your process:

1. Selection - how/why do customers choose you?
2. Point of entry - how/where do they enter your process?
3. Time to respond - how quickly do you react to their presence?
4. Point of impact - what are their first impressions?
5. Delivery - are you confident, knowledgeable, polite and *interested* in them?
6. Point of departure - did you reconfirm their requirements and satisfaction?
7. Follow up - do you have the chance for repeat business?

Source: Slack et al, Operations Management 4th Ed, 2003.
Reprinted with permission of Pearson Education Ltd.

Put yourself in your customers' shoes and 'walk through' stages 2 to 6 of your operation. What insights did this reveal? Why not survey your most valuable customers and establish what they experienced?

CHECK CUSTOMER PERCEPTION

18 DETERMINANTS OF SERVICE QUALITY

What factors determine customer perceptions of service quality?

Use of Critical Incident Technique (CIT) has helped researchers at Warwick Business School (Silvestro and Johnston) to identify 18 factors which customers generally perceive as relevant to their experience of service quality.

Extensive research in a variety of organisations supports use of the determinants in designing a comprehensive survey questionnaire to cover all aspects of the service package. This does not, however, mean a question for each determinant!

Definitions of the determinants are:

1. **Access** - how approachable the service location is; and how easy it is to find one's way around
2. **Aesthetics** - how pleasing the appearance of the service facility, goods and staff is
3. **Attentive** - how helpful/interested/willing to serve
4. **Availability** - how available facilities, staff and goods are
5. **Care** - how much concern/consideration/sympathy/patience is shown
6. **Cleanliness** - how clean/neat/tidy the appearance is of the service environment, facilities, goods, staff

CONTINUED

CHECK CUSTOMER PERCEPTION

18 DETERMINANTS OF SERVICE QUALITY

7. **Comfort**   -   how physically comfortable the service environment and facilities are

8. **Commitment**   -   how much pride/satisfaction/diligence staff show

9. **Communication** -   how clearly service providers communicate

10. **Competence**   -   how skilful/expert/professional the execution of the service is

11. **Courtesy**   -   how polite/respectful staff are in dealing with the customers and their property

12. **Flexibility**   -   how willing and able the server is to alter the service/product to meet the customer's needs

13. **Friendliness**   -   how warm and approachable contact staff are

14. **Functionality**   -   how 'fit for purpose'/serviceable the product/service/facility is

15. **Integrity**   -   how honestly/fairly customers are treated

16. **Reliability**   -   how reliable/consistent performance of staff/facilities/the service is

17. **Responsiveness** -   how fast/timely the service delivery is

18. **Security**   -   how safe the customer and his/her possessions are

Adapted from: Johnston, R (1995), The determinants of service quality: satisfiers and dissatisfiers, Int Jnl of Service Ind Management, Vol 6 No 5 pp70-71

CHECK CUSTOMER PERCEPTION

AND DON'T FORGET...

...to tap into your customers' ideas for improvement.

About the Authors

Philip Holman MA, MBA, is a Director of Awaken Consulting Limited, a consultancy that delivers efficiency improvement through people and their teams. Awaken takes best practice and translates it into practical skills for the workplace.
Tel +44 (0)1584 891578   E-mail: phil@awakenconsulting.com

Derek Snee MBA, FRSA is Director of Webster University's, Bermuda Campus and teaches on the Webster MBA. He has extensive experience of managing service operations.
Tel +441 236 4948   E-mail: sneed@webster.edu

Published by: **Management Pocketbooks Ltd**
Laurel House, Station Approach, Alresford, Hants SO24 9JH, U.K.
Tel: +44 (0)1962 735573   Fax: +44 (0)1962 733637
E-mail: sales@pocketbook.co.uk   Website: www.pocketbook.co.uk

All rights reserved © Philip Holman and Derek Snee

This edition published 2000. Reprinted 2002, 2004.   ISBN 1 870471 77 6   Printed in the U.K.

British Library Cataloguing-in-Publication Data – a catalogue record for this book is available from the British Library

ORDER FORM

Your details

Name _____

Position _____

Company _____

Address _____

_____

_____

Telephone _____

Facsimile _____

E-mail _____

VAT No. (EC companies) _____

Your Order Ref _____

Please send me:

No. copies

The Improving Efficiency Pocketbook ☐

The _____ Pocketbook ☐

The _____ Pocketbook ☐

The _____ Pocketbook ☐

The _____ Pocketbook ☐

Order by Post

MANAGEMENT POCKETBOOKS LTD
LAUREL HOUSE, STATION APPROACH, ALRESFORD,
HAMPSHIRE SO24 9JH UK

Order by Phone, Fax or Internet

Telephone: +44 (0)1962 735573
Facsimile: +44 (0)1962 733637
E-mail: sales@pocketbook.co.uk
Web: www.pocketbook.co.uk

Customers in USA should contact:
Stylus Publishing, LLC, 22883 Quicksilver Drive,
Sterling, VA 20166-2012
Telephone: 703 661 1581 or 800 232 0223
Facsimile: 703 661 1501 E-mail: styluspub@aol.com